VENIAL SIN

AN APPEAL TO ALL SORTS AND CONDITIONS OF MEN

RIGHT REV. J. S. VAUGHAN

SENSUS FIDELIUM PRESS

Print ISBN: 978-1-962639-47-7

SensusFideliumPress.com

CONTENTS

PREFACE

BY HIS EMINENCE A. CARDINAL GASQUET, O.S.B.

Bishop Vaughan's book on *Venial Sin* needs but few words of preface. The author is too well known to all to require any introduction, and the subject is so vitally important to the lives of all Catholics that it claims the attention and careful consideration of all. Unfortunately there are some—alas! I fear I should say many —who have no true perception of the evil of venial sin. They would regard mortal sins with horror, and proclaim their determination to avoid them at all cost, having no wish to offend God gravely, but at the same time they pay little attention to those lighter offences against God and his law, by which they undoubtedly offend him, although in a lesser degree. Such people probably would be horrified at the idea that they would refuse to serve him even in small things; but the truth is that they do not sufficiently appreciate the fact that in committing deliberate venial sin they are really refusing their reasonable service to God.

It is to be feared that there are not a few amongst us who flippantly declare that, whilst of course they desire to keep themselves free from any grievous offence against God, they have no particular desire to be saints, by which they mean that they regard the avoidance of every small sin as almost impossible to the ordinary man, and as only to be looked for in those whom God has called to walk in the higher paths of perfection. This notion shows how little such people remember that God has called every soul he has created to be holy—that is, to be pure and free from the stain of even small blemishes in his sight, and that every offence against his law is an evil thing which must be avoided at all cost.

God, it must never be forgotten, is always exercising an attraction on the soul he has made for himself. As the magnet draws the iron to itself, so does he draw the Christian soul to himself. Mortal sin, of course, breaks this relation with God; but venial sin weakens it, just as rust on the iron tends to partially stop the force of its attraction. It is, therefore, no light thing, from a spiritual point of view, to interpose any obstacle to God's action on the soul. Moreover, it is certain that in itself such light offences against the Almighty tend to grow, unless checked in time. Just as many maladies of the body, which in the beginning are but slight, often become grave, if not looked to in time, and, indeed, not unfrequently result in death, so the evil of venial sin, if not vigorously dealt with in the beginning, tends to grow, and indeed frequently leads to those grievous sins which kill the soul.

In fact, no deliberate venial sin can be neglected if we, even in a small degree, desire to serve God. We frequently forget how God is offended by even slight disobediences. St. Teresa was once shown the place in hell where she would have been had she not changed her life, and as far as appears there was nothing in her conduct that amounted to any mortal offence against God. So, too, St. Catherine of Siena, when she was shown how hideous venial sin made the soul in God's sight, fainted at the vision. Holy Scripture shows us also the punishment which follows on deliberate venial sin. For instance, Moses was not allowed to enter the promised land for doubting the providence of God, and David suffered great troubles for some light offence against his law.

St Francis de Sales writes very practically about the necessity of constant watchfulness in order to avoid these venial offences. He warns us that it is tempting God to have any truce with this or that evil habit, and of the necessity of waging war against our venial sins. "Aurelius," he says, "painted the faces of all his pictures like the women he loved. One who is given to fasting looks on himself as very devout, provided he fasts, though his heart is full of anger, and not daring to moisten his tongue with wine or even with water for the love of sobriety, does not hesitate to pollute it with the blood of his neighbor by detraction and calumny. Another esteems himself devout because he says a great number of prayers every day, though after he has finished he gives rein to his tongue in words that wound and are proud and injurious before his neighbors and servants.... True and living devotion, O Philothea, presupposes the love of God," and presupposes no truce with any failing. "This is why one who does not observe all the commandments of God cannot be looked on as either good or devout."

These words of St. Francis, in his *Introduction to the Devout Life*, suffice to show us the importance of avoiding even light offences against God if we desire, as with God's help we all do, to serve him and allow him to draw us to himself. This is the reason of the importance of trying to avoid even venial sins, about which this little book speaks so plainly.

A. CARD. GASQUET.
ROME,
November 27, 1923.

INTRODUCTION
BY THE AUTHOR

I once published a book entitled *Thoughts for All Times*, now in its 18th edition. The present little work might yet more appropriately be entitled *Thoughts for All Persons*. For it is not addressed to any special class, but appeals directly to every human being that has reached the use of reason. We are all, without exception, sinners. The rich and the poor, the learned and the ignorant, the old and the young, the healthy as well as the sick, all fall occasionally into venial faults, and should try to understand and to appreciate their extreme offensiveness in the sight of God.

Indeed, so great is the evil of sin, that if, through the blessing of God, this little treatise should be the means of preventing but one venial sin in any one of its readers, it will have accomplished a most glorious task, for it will have prevented an evil far greater (could one but realize it) than the Black Death, the bubonic plague, the earthquake in Tokyo, or even the universal Deluge itself. And we devoutly hope it may prevent not one only but many, and not in one only, but in many readers, which may God grant.

✠ J. S. V.

December, 1923.

1

"A venial sin may indeed appear slight, but it is an offence AGAINST GOD, and this is enough to cause it to be regarded, by one who has a right conception of that infinite Being, with greater horror than that with which he would witness the utter destruction and instant return to its original nothingness of this vast machine of the universe, with all the creatures it contains, such as the heavens, the stars, the elements, and men and angels."—*The Christian Reformed*, by B. Rogacci, S.J., p. 94.

Mortal sin is a subject very frequently treated of in Catholic pulpits, and often with considerable power and earnestness. But venial sin is scarcely ever touched upon, except incidentally and in passing. Yet it will be admitted on a little reflection that, in many respects, venial sin is a more practical and a more pressing topic, and for the following reasons:

Firstly.—Because everyone, even the good and the pious, falls into venial sins—at all events, indeliberate venial sins—whereas a very considerable number keep themselves habitually free from grosser crimes.

Secondly.—Because the opportunities of committing grievous sins are comparatively few and far between, whereas the occasions of committing venial sins are constantly arising, so that most people are guilty of them many times a day.

Thirdly.—Because there can be no doubt but that if men can only be persuaded to be really faithful and earnest in their efforts to avoid venial sin, they will run very little risk of yielding to what is so immeasurably worse. In the business of this life it is commonly said: "Take care of the pence, and the pounds will take care of themselves." In the business of the next life we may apply the same motto with even greater truth, and say with perfect confidence: "Keep away all venial sin, so far as you can, and the mortal sins will keep away of themselves."

Fourthly.—To these three reasons a fourth may be added, which deserves considerably more attention than it generally receives. It is that by speaking often of venial sin we may help as many as possible to escape, or, at all events, to diminish the amount of that truly appalling punishment in the next world which inevitably follows upon every violation of God's law, however slight, for which full satisfaction has not been made in this. Charity itself ought to be enough to induce us to warn others of the terrible consequences, which few at all realize, and to urge them to take measures to atone for their many daily offences while there is yet time.

On entering upon this very practical subject we may well begin by asking how it comes about that we Catholics, who know so well what the Church teaches on the point, do not struggle to avoid venial sin far more carefully and far more resolutely than we do. It is a most distressing and a most extraordinary, but an undeniable fact, that even pious men, and such as enjoy a well-deserved reputation for holiness, are constantly being betrayed into the commission of light faults.

They misjudge their neighbors; they entertain uncharitable thoughts; or they are testy, jealous, and exacting. They say their prayers in a distracted, inattentive, perfunctory manner. Perhaps they are easily ruffled, and have a few angry words with their wives or children or servants. They allow little things to put them out. They murmur and scold because the dinner is not properly cooked, or because the soup is cold. Or they give way to irritation because they are kept waiting at the door, or because their call has not been returned, or their pressing business letter has received no answer, or because they imagine that they have been, in some way, slighted or treated with scant courtesy and respect. Then on occasion they will tell what are called "white lies," and repeat ill-natured tales, just to amuse their neighbors.

In short, in these and in a thousand other small

ways they fall short of absolute perfection; so that day after day the impalpable dust of sin falls and gathers about their souls. I am, of course, supposing these offences to be more or less deliberate and willful, and not faults of mere frailty, surprise, or inadvertence, and I ask why even the elect, the chosen ones of God, fall so often?

It cannot possibly be due to any extreme difficulty in avoiding these little breaches of God's Law, for the simple reason that such extreme difficulty really does not exist. In fact, these very persons have often, on occasion, overcome and mastered difficulties far greater than any which these present. No. The main reason why we do not wage a more determined and a more successful warfare against such defects is that we do not really understand nor apprehend what an appalling evil venial sin is. We do not see the harm of it. We cannot fully persuade ourselves that it can possibly matter so **very, very** much whether we utter a little spiteful remark or not, or whether we yield to or resist a distraction in prayer. We know, of course, that it is better to do the right thing. But we are not at all prepared to affirm roundly and boldly that it is a most serious matter, and one calculated to affect our eternal happiness, and our relations to God himself, and to bring down upon us all kinds of disasters. No; we do not at all grasp the unspeakable evil of venial sin. In fact, we concern ourselves but very little about it. We make no serious and sustained efforts to avoid it, and this because—whatever our theory may be—

in actual practice we attach very little importance to it.

A twofold task awaits us. The first is to explain why we estimate venial sins so lightly; and the second is to point out how utterly false and fatal such an estimate is.

The chief reason why we think so lightly of venial sins is because, alas! we are so very familiar with mortal sins. Let me explain. It is a well-recognized fact that the presence of a much greater evil will always render us, in a great measure, insensible to the presence of a lesser evil. A hunter who is being devoured by a tiger does not heed—in fact, he scarcely adverts at all to—the sharp thorn, which, in the struggle, he has trodden on, and which is now actually entering his foot. He makes nothing of it. Yet, if he had nothing more serious to distract him and engage his attention, he would make a good deal of it, and declare that he was in agony, and would seek to withdraw the thorn without delay. In a somewhat similar way, one who is actually being devoured by mortal sin (or who sees others falling victims to it) is apt to think very lightly of the sharp briers and thorns of venial sin, which are tearing and lacerating the soul.

Or to employ another illustration. Just as a greater light eclipses a lesser, so a greater evil eclipses a lesser evil. Let us take an example from the physical world. Go out into the night. Look up into the sky. See how clearly and how brightly the stars are shining. Note how boldly and how prominently they stand out against the dark background. Anyone who can see at all can see these brilliantly gleaming points. But now take up your stand on exactly the same spot in the daytime. Look up into the cloudless blue on a summer morning when the sun is flooding the heavens with its golden rays. Are the stars still there? Of course they are! They are scattered in hundreds and thousands over the whole expanse. True; but do they stand out clearly, as during the darkest night? Can you see them distinctly; or rather, let me ask, can you see them at all? No! Not a trace of them remains. Why? Because the immeasurably greater brilliance of the sun wholly hides and eclipses them. They are there, as they always are, and they have lost none of their beauty, yet they no longer produce the slightest impression on our eyes. The intense light of the sun has rendered them invisible. Could you put an extinguisher on the sun for a moment, every star would reappear, and be seen twinkling and glittering for you again; but, release the sun once more, and again the stars disappear just as before.

Now, I take it that something analogous takes place in the spiritual order. Mortal sin is so inconceivably great an evil that, by comparison, venial sin seems scarcely to be evil at all. Just as a great light renders it difficult to measure the brightness of a lesser light, or even to perceive it at all, so our familiarity with a greater evil will cause us to think little of a lesser evil, or perhaps not to regard it as an evil at all.

Through the mercy of God, many of us have, perhaps, never once, during the whole course of our lives, fallen into mortal sin. But even then, there can be no doubt but that we are familiar with it; that is to say, we are perfectly well aware that it is being committed by thousands of persons every day. We can never take up a paper without meeting cases of theft, of murder, of suicide, of drunkenness, and of fighting and quarrelling and the rest. We are not only horrified, but unfortunately the result often is that we are disposed to reserve all our indignation, loathing, hatred, and execration for mortal sin; while we grow somewhat tolerant and even indulgent of venial sin, and very likely say that we would feel quite satisfied "if the people did nothing worse." And, of course, in a way, we are right. For mortal sin is, in very truth, immeasurably worse than venial. It is inexpressively more odious and loathsome in itself, and inexpressibly more disastrous and fatal in its consequences. So that we are bound to admit that by comparison venial sin looks, and indeed is, very insignificant indeed. When placed side by side with that hellish monster, the vileness and ingratitude of venial sin seem to disappear, as the light of the stars before the greater light of the noonday sun.

But this is the utmost that can be alleged on behalf of venial sin. Once we have declared that it is not so hateful and abominable as mortal sin, we have said absolutely all that even the strongest advocate could possibly urge in its favor. But in itself—and it is in itself that we must consider it—it is by far the most hideous and hateful thing imaginable, and to be opposed, fought against, resisted, wrestled with, and execrated with the utmost industry and determination. If, for the moment, we put mortal sin altogether out of our calculation, we may affirm, without hesitation and without the slightest exaggeration, that there is literally no evil whatsoever so great as venial sin. There are evils of all kinds existing in the world, or what worldly men, at all events, call evils, such as poverty, disgrace, disease, wounds, misfortunes, losses, agonies, death, and so forth. Yet none of these evils, however distressing and galling, contain a fraction of the evil that lies concentrated in one venial sin.

Sadly do we deceive ourselves when we try to palliate our venial faults and slur them over, because we allow ourselves to be led by our imagination rather than by our reason. Setting aside, then, our imagination, let us apply our reason. Faith tells us that the Catholic Church is the Oracle of God, the mouthpiece of Jesus Christ. We know, with absolute certainty, that when she opens her mouth she speaks the infallible truth; and that she is incapable of overstating or of in any way exaggerating Christ's doctrine. Now, keeping this well in mind, we proceed to ask what exactly she teaches regarding the present point. She teaches that:

1. Every venial sin is an offence against God.

2. That no circumstance or motive whatsoever can ever justify a person committing it.

3. That a man is bound to embrace any other alternative, however painful and however difficult and distressing, rather than incur the guilt of venial sin.

4. And that it is, in all cases, an insult, offered by a contemptible nothing, to the Infinite Majesty of God.

As Cardinal Newman expresses it in his own incomparable way: "The Church holds that it were better for sun and moon to drop from Heaven, for the earth to fail, and for all the many millions who are on it to die of starvation, in extremest agony (as far as temporal affliction goes), than that one soul, *I will not say should be lost, but should commit one single venial sin.*"[1]

Hence, if we might escape the most agonizing disease, ending in an excruciating death, by yielding to a small venial sin, we should unhesitatingly choose agony and death. If by giving way to such a fault we could ward off pestilence, famine, fire, sword, earthquakes, and inundations, which otherwise would destroy every living soul from one end of the world to the other, it would be absolutely sinful and impious for us to commit it, and we should be justly punished were we to yield to the temptation.

Why? Because no evil, no accumulation of evils, no continuation of evils, provided that sin is not included amongst them, can equal the evil which is contained in even the least moral fault. Nay, more, so immeasurable is the evil of venial sin, that it would be wrong to consent to it, even though by its means we could convert all heretics and infidels, bring all sinners to repentance, empty Purgatory, and restore the lost in hell to grace and salvation. Yea, even if we were able to secure to all men, present, past, and future, the joys and delights of the Beatific Vision, we are bound to declare bluntly and emphatically and without hesitation that such an act of venial sin must not be permitted.

Why? Because it is so horrible an evil that the worst privations, suffered by all living creatures, are as nothing compared to it. But there is no use multiplying comparisons, since, whatever the physical or material evils may be, they can never approach the degree of evil contained in a single venial sin.

This is not an "opinion." It is a certain fact. It is not a view; nor the teaching of some particular school. No! It is a dogma of our holy Faith. It is terrible! Undoubtedly. But it is true. It is incomprehensible, and my reason sits uneasily under the doctrine. Certainly it is incomprehensible and hard to bear. But, again, we repeat it is true. That, after all, is the important point.

There are many truths hard to believe in our holy religion. There are many mysteries, and of them all sin is, perhaps, one of the most difficult. But we are bound to accept these revealed truths, all the same. Our reason is limited. Being finite, it is incompetent to deal with every supernatural revelation. God himself is a mystery to us, and all his thoughts deeper than any human plummet can sound. "O the depth of the riches of the wisdom and of the knowledge of God! How incomprehensible are his judgements! How unsearchable are his ways!"[2] exclaims St. Paul.

Though this doctrine is of Faith, yet, if once we admit the existence of an infinitely perfect God, it may be shown to be according to sound reason as well as to Faith. Thus sin, even venial sin, is an offence offered to God. All other evils, of whatever kind, are offences offered to creatures. But since God is *infinitely* exalted above creatures, it follows that the least insult or injury offered to God is a greater evil than the greatest offered to his creatures. Let us clothe our argument in the folds of a parable.

A mighty and perfect king, while strolling through his domains one day, chanced to dip the point of his finger into the waters of a stagnant pond. On withdrawing it, he notices a tiny drop adhering to it. Now, in that drop, let us suppose, there are millions and millions of living creatures: infusoria, protozoa, and the like. It is true you cannot see them with the naked eye, but they are there. In fact, the little drop is more thickly populated by these minute creatures than the world is populated by human beings.

Now, which act would be considered the greater evil, an act which would destroy the life of this wise and noble king, or an act which would destroy the lives of every inhabitant of that rain-drop world? There can be no doubt as to what the answer would be. But go a step further and ask, which would be the greater evil, an act by which the king should lose, not his life, but merely his sight, or his hearing, or one of his limbs or organs, or, on the other hand, an act by which the entire microscopic world of infusoria should be utterly annihilated? Again there would be no hesitation in our reply. Why is this? Because a wise and noble king, or indeed, any human being, stands so far above and so immensely superior to an animalcule, that it would be better that millions should perish altogether than that a single man should ever experience any pain, hurt, or even any slight inconvenience.

The application of this fable is clear enough. All creatures, both angelic and human—in short, the whole universe of being—are not only less, but infinitely less, when compared to God, than a drop full of animalcules is, when compared to a man. Between the mightiest monarch and the smallest of invisible animalcules the distance is, after all, not infinite; but between God and even the highest of the Cherubim or Seraphim the distance is absolutely infinite and inconceivable.

As a consequence, the slightest injury done to God must be immeasurably worse *in se* than any conceivable injury done to man or angel. So that, in itself, it would be far better and more desirable that all men should be in pain than that God alone should be in any way offended: that all creatures should perish than that God should be in any way slighted or contradicted.

This, then, is the doctrine of the Church of God. We have to accept it, not as a speculative truth, not as a theory, but as a profound fact, which touches us most nearly and most personally. What, then, are we to think of a person who professes to believe venial sin to be so gigantic an evil, and so outrageous an insult, and yet who takes little or no pains to avoid it? What estimate shall we make of a man's sincerity when, on the one hand, we hear him affirm that death and disgrace are infinitely to be preferred to the slightest sin, while, on the other hand, we see him yielding to such sins on the slightest provocation, while he will make any sacrifices to ward off the approach of death, or even of poverty or disease? Surely our faith ought to control our conduct, and direct and shape our lives. And, no doubt, it would do so if it were a vivid faith; if, in a word, we were more fully conscious of its teaching, and more keenly anxious to obey its voice.

Go back over your past lives. Summon your past experience to your aid, and ask yourself: When I chattered away so glibly with so and so, and defamed such a one, and criticized or found fault with such another, or prevaricated in order to exalt myself, or to depreciate a rival, or when I "economized" the truth to serve ignoble ends; or when I was guilty of other venial offences, was I at all conscious of what I was doing? Did I advert to the fact that I was, in very truth, the real and the sole cause of a greater calamity and of a worse evil than is the earthquake, that swallows up whole cities; than the plague, or the Black Death, that slays its many millions; or than the cruel waters of the Deluge, which drowned an entire world? No, perhaps not, but as a matter of simple fact I was really guilty of a far worse evil. Where, oh! where is our faith? Can we accept such a doctrine and go on sinning? Can we acknowledge venial sin to be all we have said, and indeed, more than we have said, and yet continue to give way to it on the slightest pretext?

To witness the ease with which even good and holy men succumb, one might indeed suppose that their Faith had grown very defective, or that they had ceased altogether to believe. But perhaps the truer explanation is not that they do not believe, but that they fail to reflect, to realize, and heartily to acknowledge to themselves what the Church actually teaches.

Alas! It is too true. We find difficulty in judging aright, and can hardly be persuaded to see things as God sees them, because we are still so imperfect, and in such spiritual darkness. "The sensual man perceiveth not the things that are of the Spirit of God; for it is foolishness to him" (1 Cor. 2:14). Well may holy David ask: *Delicta quis intelligit?*

But the nearer we approach to God, and the more brightly the light of grace burns in our hearts, the more shall we come to understand the filth and fetidness of venial sin, and the more carefully and the more successfully shall we wage a relentless war against our daily faults and imperfections.

Let us, then, apply ourselves to the important task earnestly and without delay, for the years are hurrying by, and the day of life is already far spent, and the night is fast approaching, when no man can work.

2

"For as the righteous man often falls in a day, as the Wise one says, it is not believable how various are the imperfections of those beginning. Those which torment more, are venial sins; for although the righteous persevere in grace, it is not believable how much venial sins hinder the perfection of charity and intimate union with God."—Vide Compen. Theo. Ascet. Myst., by Cardinal Vives, O.M.Cap., p. 116.

I suppose all, without so much as one exception, who have given the matter their serious consideration, will admit that none of us *sufficiently* estimates, in practice, the seriousness and the intrinsic malignity of deliberate venial sin. This utter want of anything approaching a due appreciation of its malice and deformity arises from various causes.

I. We have already considered, in our first chapter,

what we take to be the chief cause; but there are others which also deserve mentioning.

II. The *second* cause is our unfortunate familiarity with venial faults. It is said that *familiarity breeds contempt*. This is especially true in the case before us. The majority of people get so accustomed to follow nature rather than grace, and to give way to whatever inclination comes uppermost, so long as the matter is not grievous, that at last they scarcely advert to the innumerable little offences and lesser violations of God's law of which they are guilty. Very few take the trouble even to think about them, or to make them a subject of serious examination. The very fact that they are perpetually being betrayed into small infidelities, renders them almost insensible of them. This, unfortunately, seems to be a law of our nature.

III. A *third* reason is because, although we sin and sin again and again venially, yet no harm seems to come of it. The fault and its punishment do not follow one another at once. Nothing happens to compel us to feel the malice of it so soon as ever it is committed. In former times God was wont—from time to time—to visit the offender with immediate and condign punishment. Because Moses doubted for a moment, when God told him to strike the rock and that water would gush out, he is thought to have been guilty of a mere venial offence, yet he was, there and then, most severely punished. For he was forbidden to enter the Promised Land, towards which he had been slowly and anxiously approaching for forty years, and had then almost reached, and which was already in sight.

We have another case, in the person of Zachary, the father of St. John the Baptist. As a punishment of one little venial sin he was struck both deaf and dumb.

Even the sin of Ananias and Saphira, who told a lie about some land they had bought, is not thought, by many commentators, to have been more than venial, yet, on account of that lie, first Ananias was struck down dead, and then, almost immediately afterwards, his wife Saphira. How few would tell lies as readily as they do now, if such summary punishment were general in these days!

Or take another case. Mary, the sister of Moses, began to murmur against him, and spoke ill of him, and behold, God caused her to be immediately punished by leprosy, so that the Scripture tells us, "Behold, Mary appeared white as snow with leprosy" (Num. 12:10).

How different things would be in these days, if every uncharitable thought and every unkind word were to engender, as soon as uttered, some very painful and loathsome disease which would rack our nerves with pain! But such is not God's method. His punishment for venial sin is far worse than any leprosy, but he reserves it for another world. We shall understand something of the evil of venial sin when we are burning amid the purging flames of Purgatory. But one of the reasons of our present carelessness in avoiding slight offences is because, during this life, we may commit them with apparent impunity.

IV. A *fourth* cause is the utterly false view taken of venial sin by the world around us. Man is very much affected, as a rule, by the views, opinions, and judgements of those among whom he lives. Whether he reads the papers, or magazines, or books, or whether he converses with friends and companions, or merely listens to them talk—and exchanging views with one another, he will realize how very few attach the smallest importance to slight sins. Now, he does not claim to be wiser or more enlightened than others, and has a very convenient way of accepting their estimate of most things. He finds that sin is a very small evil in their eyes, or perhaps none at all. They refer to it without horror, call it by soft names, and laugh and joke about it, as though it were unworthy of serious thought. In fact, the world, as Cardinal Newman observes, thinks sin "the same sort of imperfection as an impropriety, or a want of taste, or infirmity," and nothing more.

And, as we are living in the world, and mixing with all sorts and conditions of men, we shall find ourselves, almost inadvertently, adopting their judgements, unless, arousing ourselves to a sense of our danger, we take prompt steps to neutralize it. But, "Quis est hic, et laudabimus eum? Fecit enim mirabilia in vita sua."

In order to be really secure, we must be constantly correcting inwardly the false teaching of the world, and calling to mind the true doctrine of the infallible witness to God's eternal Truth.

Now, setting aside for the moment all question of mortal sin, we have already considered that venial sin is the very greatest of all possible evils, and that literally no greater calamity could possibly befall us than to be stricken with the stain of even one deliberate venial sin.

Let us now call to mind the fact that it is according to God's plan, and a law of his infinite justice, that no one shall "work iniquity" without reaping the consequences. If I yield deliberately to so much as one single venial fault, I thereby not only commit evil, but, at the same time, I do myself a very serious injury. In consequence of this offence, I shall suffer in this life and I shall suffer in the next. For the present, we will confine our remarks to some of the more notable consequences that follow venial sin in this world.

A.—The first of these is that it darkens the intellect and clouds the judgement concerning the things of God. Just as there is night and day in the physical order, so there is night and day in the spiritual order. Now what the sun is in the material world, that God is in the spiritual world. He is the "Sun of Justice," "the true light, which enlighteneth every man that cometh into this world" (John 1:9). But God does not scatter his gifts equally upon all. His light shines with far greater brilliance in the heart of the saint than in the heart of the sinner. The freer the soul is from sin, and the purer it is from every defect, the more fully the light of God enters into it, and the more far-reaching and perfect its vision becomes. It is as it is with material light. Thus, though the sun may shine with exactly the same power on two different windows, yet the amount of light entering them may be absolutely different. If the window-panes be perfectly clean and spotless the sun will enter freely, and so flood the whole room with its light that those within it will be able to see every object with the utmost clearness; but if the window be covered with dust and dirt and begrimed with the accumulated deposits of years, the rays of light will indeed beat upon it as before, but with very little effect. Little, if any, light will enter, and the hideousness and the fetor, even of the most filthy objects, will be scarcely distinguishable. Such is a fair picture of a soul stained with a multitude of venial faults and failings. These, by reason of their being "deeds of darkness," obscure the light of the Holy Spirit, so that (even with the best will in the world) a soul so circumstanced *utterly fails to realize the full enormity* even of the gravest sin, and so will fall much more easily and much more deeply than those who keep their consciences pure and free from even the smallest defects.

"Ordinary Christians [says Father Bowden] are aware, probably, of habitual falls into venial sins of the coarser kind, but of the subtler workings of their self-love and of spiritual sins they know little or nothing. The saints, on the other hand, search their souls by the light of God's perfections. *One ray of his eternal purity entering their hearts discloses*, as *horrible deformities, their least defects*, while the closeness of their relations to him shows these defects to be a personal outrage on the divine Majesty. Before the eyes of a saint, thus enlightened, the all-holy God is not only their Creator and Lawgiver, but the one Being on whose influx and support they depend for every vital action; according to the words of the Apostle: 'In him we live and move and are.' From this arises their sense of the hideous malice of sin."[1]

There can be no doubt but that a soul who is careful to abstain as far as possible from every imperfection, however small, that can offend God, is a soul that has drawn very near to him, who is the Sun of Justice, and this divine Sun sheds such a penetrating light within his heart that he becomes *extremely sensitive to the least defect*, and can, in a measure, recognize more clearly than others, not only the presence, but also the loathsomeness of faults, which otherwise would be scarcely noticed, or perhaps not be reckoned as offences at all!

"We do not know what sin is [writes Cardinal Newman] because we do not know what God is; we have no standard with which to compare it till we know what God is. Only God's glories, his perfections, his holiness, his majesty, his beauty, can teach us, by the contrast, how to think of sin; and (since we do not see God here), till we see him we cannot form a just judgement of what sin is; till we enter heaven we must take what God tells us of sin mainly on faith. Nay, even then we shall be able to condemn sin only so far as we are able to see and praise and glorify God; he alone can duly judge of sin who can comprehend God; he only judged of sin according to the *fulness* of its evil, who, knowing the Father from eternity with a perfect knowledge, showed what he thought of sin by dying for it; he only, who was willing, though he was God, to suffer inconceivable pains of soul and body in order to make satisfaction for it. Take his word, or rather his deed, for the truth of this awful doctrine—that a single mortal sin is enough to cut you off from God for ever.[2]

And let me add, that a single *venial* sin is enough to cut you off from the full possession of God, in the Beatific Vision, so long at least as it is not fully repented of and atoned for.

If there be anyone in this world who can form some appreciable estimate of the heinousness of venial sin, it is only the pure of heart, for they alone are given the grace, according to the text: "Blessed are the pure of heart, for they shall see God." Just as one of the rewards of perfect innocence and freedom, even from venial sin, is a wonderful sense of the holiness of God and of his unapproachable sanctity, so one of the punishments of venial sins and imperfections is a diminution of that sense and a spiritual blindness, which causes us to minimize its evil.

B.—But deliberate venial sins bring upon us a second punishment. They render the will less vigorous in resisting temptation, so that one who habitually yields to even small faults will yield far more easily to serious sins than one who is more faithful. This is easy to understand, for the will, like any other faculty, is susceptible of education. Its powers are drawn out, strengthened and developed by exercise. It may be trained either to resist its attractions or to follow them blindly. In itself the will is most plastic and malleable, so that it may be molded in this way or in that, according to our good pleasure. And, if we accustom ourselves to resist and to overcome our inordinate inclinations, the effort grows easier and easier as time goes on. Man is essentially a creature of habit; and habit is the result of constant repetition. In fact, without repetition we cannot form a habit. This is true in every department of life. Take the first stone-carrier or bricklayer you meet on the road, and set him down in front of a grand piano. Place his hands on the keyboard, and ask him, I will not say to play, but merely to run his fingers rapidly and smoothly up and down the scales. Impossible! As well ask him to talk Hebrew. But why? Surely it cannot be so extremely difficult in itself, for even the little school-girl will acquit herself of the task with the greatest ease. No; it is not so very hard. *With a little practice* it is easy enough, but remember this, without *practice* it is not only difficult but impossible.

Practice makes the joints supple and ready to obey the slightest behest of the will, so that the fingers glide to and fro, and from bass to treble and from treble to bass, over the keys, as though to nature born. Now it is very much the same thing with regard to the will. The will, almost spontaneously and of itself, will learn to resist evil and do good, just as the fingers will learn how to perform with skill upon the piano. But it is essential that I take my will in hand, and carefully cultivate it. I must teach it and instruct it. I must exercise it, every day and many times a day, in the most important art of resisting and conquering my evil inclinations in small things. To acquire a perfect command of any musical instrument whatsoever, one has to take trouble, and to spend time, and to go through the exercises and to practice assiduously. And, what is more, thousands are quite ready to submit to this drudgery and to brace themselves up to the task, merely to become perfect masters of the piano, or the organ, or the violin. Surely we should be ready and anxious to do as much, and far more, in order to grow perfect in the service of God and in the practice of virtue?

If I am constantly checking myself, and denying myself, and curbing my passions, and restraining my desires, and suppressing my evil inclinations, and bridling my tongue, and keeping a guard over my eyes, etc., etc., I am not only exercising virtue (which is an exceedingly important thing), but I am doing much more. I am actually engaged in forming a habit which will be of immense and, indeed, of incalculable service to me in my spiritual warfare. I am doing a truly admirable thing. I am laying the foundations of true sanctity; that is to say, I am forming a habit which will be ever strengthening my will, and rendering it more robust and better able to resist temptation. I am training it to conquer, and fitting it for more certain and greater victories. Yes; literally, I am training as an athlete trains for a race, or as a musician practices for a display on the piano.

Surely it must be quite evident that one who zealously and perseveringly strives to overcome venial sin is—from the very nature of the case—always exercising his will in the right direction, and establishing it more and more firmly in virtue. What is the result? The result is, that when some really serious and dangerous temptation assails him, he will make short work of it, and gain a most glorious victory. His will, being inured to resistance and thoroughly well trained in the art of self-denial, will run no real risk, but will achieve an easy, a speedy, and a most decisive triumph. He will bear down his adversary, as one quite familiar to the task: much as a boxer, *in full training*, will floor an inexperienced neophyte who should dare to attack him.

Compare such a true soldier of Jesus Christ with the easy-going, careless self-indulgent, and listless Christian, who deems it quite enough to restrain himself from mortal sin. Such a cowardly and unworthy follower of Christ yields himself up to his desires, so long as they demand nothing grievously wrong. He is afraid of hell and resolves to escape the quenchless flames, for if he have no very exalted love of God, he has a most exaggerated love of himself. But he has no very strong hatred and abhorrence of lesser offences. He makes no attempt to repress little sallies of temper, little fits of jealousy, harsh or uncharitable words, or proud and ambitious thoughts. He will not hesitate to tell what he calls a "white lie" in order to excuse himself, and will retire to bed, if very tired, without saying his night prayers, and will (without getting actually drunk) indulge far too freely in champagne or whisky. Now observe. He too is training his will. Yes, alas! He is training it to yield; and practicing it all the day long in the art not of self-restraint but of self-indulgence. In a word, he too (whether he adverts to it or not) is diligently forming and fostering a habit —that horrible habit of sin.

What is the consequence? His will becomes enfeebled and languid, and by long custom yields most readily to every evil suggestion, and can hardly ever be induced to do anything so unusual and formidable as to resist serious temptation. In fact, being trained so assiduously and for so long to indulge its inclination in lesser things, the will feels quite unmanned and helpless in the presence of the much more violent and powerful temptation, and knows not how to oppose it. A man who will not resist trifling acts of dishonesty, and who cannot keep his fingers off pence or shillings when they lie in his way, is not likely to keep them off pounds and banknotes when the opportunity arises.

There are two warnings given us in this connection. The one is an axiom of human wisdom and observation, viz., *Nemo repente summus*. No one becomes wicked all at once. If this be true, then, we may be sure that a person who habitually shuns small faults will not suddenly drop into grievous ones. It is only he who begins to give way in little things, and who allows himself certain unlawful liberties, who, at length, sinks into deadly sins, wrecks his whole life, and "purchases for himself damnation."

The second warning to which I have referred is of yet greater importance, as it comes to us with the infallible authority of the Holy Ghost. He distinctly declares, by the lips of Ecclesiasticus (19:1) that "He who contemneth small things, shall fall by little and little."

Small sins pave the way for more serious ones. To use a common expression, they introduce the thin end of the wedge, which may then be more easily driven right in, to our serious discomfiture. They may be compared to the fissures and splits in an otherwise worthy vessel. They let the tide in, which may at last sink the whole ship, with all its valuable cargo, and send it to the bottom.

I. There are some very foolish persons who calmly make up their minds to avoid mortal sin, while reserving to themselves full liberty to commit as many venial sins as they please.

In this they utterly deceive themselves. It is impossible to carry out such a resolve. To hit the bull's-eye on a target you must point your arrow, not at it, but above it. In like manner, to succeed in avoiding all mortal sin, it will not suffice to aim at avoiding mortal sin only. We must aim higher. We must resolve to avoid, so far as we can, all deliberate venial sin also. Otherwise we shall share the fate of the Italian coach driver on the Alps, who argued that it mattered nothing how near to the edge of the precipice the wheels might go, provided they did not go beyond the edge. Till at last, one day, attempting to illustrate this theory, he somewhat miscalculated the distance, the result of which was that he and his coach and all in it suddenly disappeared into the abyss. A similar fate awaits all those who hover around as near to the very brink of mortal sin as they think they can get. Like the too venturesome moth, pirouetting around the flaring gas-jet, they get burnt to death when they least expect it. So much for the **FIRST** punishment that follows upon deliberate venial sin.

II. Now let us consider the second. The habit of committing venial sin not only weakens our will and darkens our understanding, but it also increases the violence and the strength of our spiritual enemies, by which I mean our passions, sinful desires, and evil inclinations. Our unmortified propensities may be compared to those tiny little sparks of fire which are found in a brazier full of burning charcoal. Though they be indeed but sparks, yet they possess much latent power. If you merely fan them, as I have often seen Italian servants do, they begin to glow more and more brightly. If you continue to blow upon them ever so softly, they, all of a sudden, cease to be sparks and break into flame, and finally produce a regular conflagration which there is no managing or controlling. In like manner, small passions easily grow by little indulgences, until they become almost irresistible. A story is told of a certain Indian chief who, having shot a fine lioness, took compassion on her tiny little cub, and brought it home and made a pet of it. So long as it remained a mere cub he experienced no difficulty in dealing with it. But as he kept on feeding it day by day it became stronger and stronger, until at last, in a fit of anger, it one day rushed at its benefactor and tore him to pieces. So is it with our passions. While they are still incipient and undeveloped, we may keep them within bounds, but so soon as we begin to feed them—that is to say, so soon as we give them what they crave for, and indulge their appetite—they develop and grow stronger and stronger, till at last they will master us and bring about our downfall. Suppose a case.

A man over-indulges in drink. He does not get actually *drunk*, but takes frequently more than he ought. He is feeding the lioness's whelp. In this way he strengthens it. At last, a day comes when the inclination proves too strong for him, and he sins grievously. The whelp has torn him to pieces (spiritually). Or a man may feel the promptings of some impure desire. He begins by allowing himself some slight liberties. He becomes a little venturesome and imprudent. In a word, he feeds this whelp of Satan, this evil passion, till, growing stronger and stronger by each indulgence, it, so to speak, falls upon him at last, and tears him to pieces; in other words, destroys the life of grace in his soul.

Thus it is evident that habitual venial sin produces two most disastrous effects at one and the same time.

On the one hand it strengthens our temptations, and on the other it weakens our will, and makes us far less able to resist them. In other words, it gives our enemies greater power to harm us, while it reduces our power of resistance. These consequences are bad enough, but this is not all.

III. In the third place, venial sin also deprives us of that special and altogether exceptional friendship which God is ever ready to show to those who are aiming at perfection. This constitutes the **THIRD** punishment of such offences. All masters of the spiritual life are agreed that, by our small infidelities and self-indulgence, we forfeit all right to God's choicest and highest favors and blessings. It is true that he gives *enough* to all. All may reckon upon receiving his ordinary graces. But, in addition to that, there are a vast number of rare and indeed priceless graces which he reserves for his more dutiful and obedient children. On these he is wont to confer innumerable spiritual gifts and helps, which he withholds from those whose carelessness and lukewarmness in his service have rendered them wholly undeserving. God defends and protects in some measure every soul that calls upon him, but he has an altogether special love for such as are aiming at a yet closer union with him, and these he watches over and guards, as the "very apple of his eye" (*ut pupillam oculi*).

What the exact measure of this loss may be, in any particular case, none of us shall know until we enter into the next world, and learn exactly how far short we are of having reached the exalted position to which we might have attained had we shown a little more zeal.

Venial sin deprives us of God's **special** favors. We do not say that it extinguishes divine grace. No! Thank God! That it can never do. Whether our soul be stained by one or by a thousand or by a hundred thousand venial offences, they can never deprive it altogether of the friendship of almighty God. Venial sins do not coalesce like other things. It is true that twelve pence will make a shilling, and that 160 stone weight will make one ton; but no number of venial sins, however they may be multiplied, can ever make or equal one mortal sin, nor convert God from a friend into an enemy, as mortal sin does.

IV. What other effect, then, have venial sins upon the soul? They disfigure its beauty, they bespatter it with moral filth, they stain it, they wound it, they render it so unsightly and hideous that it can never be admitted into heaven so long as they remain adhering to it. But it is still alive with the life of divine grace, though its vitality is much enfeebled. God's attitude towards such a soul may be compared to a loving mother's attitude towards her own sick child. The child may be ill, and its poor little body weakened by disease, and covered with pustules and pimples and festering ulcers and running scars, but she loves it still and cherishes it, as only a mother can. She will no longer press it to her bosom, nor smother it with kisses, because its flesh is one mass of filthy scabs, but she will not cast it off from her, nor utterly despise it.

No; her attitude is still one of gentleness, compassion, and even of love. When the poor little body is not only unsightly, but absolutely cold and dead, she tearfully submits to be separated from it. She allows the strange hands to be laid upon her child, and the infant corpse to be taken away from her, and to be flung into the grave, out of her sight for ever.

So in the case of Almighty God. No venial sin, however horrid and loathsome it may be in his sight, can cause him to withdraw his love. It is only when mortal sin has actually destroyed the life of grace, that he allows strangers—*i.e.*, the demons—to claim their victims, and to take final possession of the guilty soul. On the other hand, no one can form any conception of the deformity of venial sin, or understand how it lays waste the beauty of the soul. Nor can anyone realize the injury a soul does itself by such carelessness and remissness in corresponding with the ever available grace of God, which would have protected it from all evil. God has sometimes, as we read in the lives of his saints, brought the image of a single venial sin before them as it appears in the light of his countenance, and they tell us that the sight did all but kill them, nay, would have killed them, had it not been instantly withdrawn.[3] If we cannot actually see the full deformity and malice of venial sin as such favored souls have seen it, let us at least stir up our faith and believe it fully, and so merit a more special blessing from our divine Lord, on the strength of our being among those who, though they "have not seen, yet have believed" (John 20:29).

We may foolishly try and persuade ourselves that it is a trifling thing to avoid venial sins. Yet it is such "trifles that make perfection," and as Michael Angelo said, "perfection is no trifle"!

3

"We are guilty, without a doubt; we greatly offend the good Lord; but are we not always, thanks to His mercy, at the sources of forgiveness?"—Cardinal Mercier, A mes Séminaristes, p. 241.

One of the most lamentable consequences of the Fall of our first parents is our own extraordinary propensity to sin. So strong is the inclination that there is no one, however careful he may be, who can altogether overcome it. With the exception of the most Blessed Virgin Mary, who *singulari Dei privilegio* was shielded from even the very shadow of sin, the entire human race has been contaminated by the slime of the serpent, so that there is not one grown-up man or woman who can claim complete exemption even from actual personal sin.

This seems an appalling statement, but the inspired words of Holy Scripture are far too precise and explicit to make it possible to deny it. "There is no one who sinneth not," it declares in one place. In another place it says: "In many things we all offend." While St. John puts the case yet more emphatically, for in his Epistle he writes: "If we say that we have no sin, we deceive ourselves, and the truth is not in us" (1 John 1:8).

Is it, then, we may well ask, absolutely impossible to keep from all sin? Here we must distinguish. It is, no doubt, possible to keep from all mortal sin. In fact, one may certainly say that many saints (the canonized and the uncanonized) have lived and died without ever forfeiting their baptismal innocence, or losing the grace of God, by any grievous sin.

But is it possible to attain the full use of reason, and then live on, year in year out, without ever falling into *venial*[1] sin? Here again a distinction must be made. It is practically impossible to avoid all sins of surprise, of frailty, and of inadvertence and so forth, but most learned theologians admit that we really have the power, if only we have the will, to avoid all *deliberate* faults. It is very important to bear in mind that the difference in malice between a deliberate and an indeliberate offence is almost immeasurable. Our free human will is the great source both of merit and demerit. In judging both vice and virtue we may truly say, *everything depends upon the will*. Exclude the will wholly and entirely, and there can be no sin whatsoever. And the less concerned the will is in any bad action, the less accountable are we for it, and the less guilty we stand in the sight of God. Hence it follows that in many sins of frailty and surprise, in which the action of the will is exceedingly slight, and indeed often next to nothing, such offences are scarcely deserving of the name of sins and are generally spoken of rather as imperfections.

But if we cannot avoid all venial sin, do we at least make a serious and sustained effort, commensurate with the importance of the subject, to reduce their number to a minimum? It will be well to examine our attitude of mind, (1) before, and (2) during, and (3) after temptation.

Before.—Do we live in an habitual state of dread lest we should be betrayed into the commission of some venial offence? Do we excite within ourselves a strong habitual detestation and energetic hatred of all such offences? Do we in very truth regard them really and truly as immeasurably worse than disease, or death, or any other purely earthly calamity? Do we, as so many of the saints did, pray most earnestly to God that he would mercifully take us out of this world rather than permit us to be guilty of venial sin? It is related of St. Alphonsus Rodriguez that whenever he went out for a walk he would first commend himself to God, and then pray most fervently that he would cause him to fall dead at the threshold rather than offend him by any slight sin.

Rev. Father John Morris, S.J., observes: "The punishment of venial sin is closely akin to that of mortal sin, excepting the eternity, and therefore the despair. Both have pain of sense proportionate to the malice with which the creature was preferred to the Creator; and though there is no aversion from God in venial sin, both have a real loss of God, though that of venial sin is only for a time."

That must be an exceedingly great evil, exclaims Père Chaignon, S.J., which cannot be repaired by the tears of the whole world, by the torments of the martyrs, the austerities of the anchorites, the mortifications of all the saints, nor by all the good works that have been performed by holy men from the beginning of the world until now, and that shall be performed from now to the end of time. Yet all these satisfactions united would not suffice to repair the outrage against God caused by one single venial sin, if we had not the infinite satisfactions of God-made-man to add to them and to give them their value.[2] By virtue of the graces and merits which the Passion and death of our divine Lord have purchased for us, we are given the power to atone for, and to merit forgiveness, but *apart from the infinite satisfactions of Jesus Christ*, we should be in a hopeless condition and wholly incapable of offering adequate satisfaction even for our venial faults.

"Not all the zeal and labors of the Apostles, nor all the blood of the martyrs, nor the penances and prayers of the confessors, nor the chastity of the virgins: not all the merits of the Virgin Queen of heaven herself could make adequate satisfaction. . . . All these merits, great as they are, could not, of their own value, satisfy for a *single deliberate venial sin*."[3]

Once we perceive the seriousness of venial sin, and its true nature and deformity, we shall certainly become more watchful and circumspect, and will not only guard ourselves against the occasions, but will pray very much more earnestly to be protected and defended against all the fiery shafts of the most wicked one.

During the Temptation.—So soon as ever we become conscious of the presence of temptation, we should at once strive to realize the gravity and the awful seriousness of what the tempter is asking us to do. Then we should lift up our thoughts and hearts to God, and implore him most earnestly to protect us, and so to strengthen our will that we may refuse all consent. The more vividly we recall all that has been said concerning the immensity of the offence in the eyes of God, and its deplorable consequences, the less likely are we to give way. We sin generally because we do not weigh the gravity of even the slightest venial offence.

After we have given way.—Should we be conscious that we have really stained our souls with venial sin, we should be filled with shame and sorrow, and feel how basely and unworthily we have acted, and most humbly beg God's pardon. Instead of dismissing the fault as "merely venial," and attaching but little importance to it, we should strive to understand how disgracefully and ungratefully we have behaved, and how thoroughly we have deserved God's awful punishments. We should convince ourselves that what we have done is so truly abominable and hateful in his sight, that our only hope of forgiveness lies in the *infinite* merits of the incarnate God and his sacred death and Passion.

On this, most fortunately, we are able to rely with the greatest confidence. In fact, if sin is such a gigantic evil, so that it would be difficult to exaggerate it, on the other hand, God, in his infinite mercy and compassion, has made it exceedingly easy for us to erase every trace of it from our souls. But, alas! such is our blindness and folly, that even though innumerable venial sins stain our soul, we scarcely make any adequate and sustained effort to free ourselves from them. If the saints, like ourselves, were always falling into slight faults, they were also always making every effort to atone for them. By their prayers, their tears, their frequent fastings and watchings and constant mortifications, they sought to purify their souls, and to render them wholly pure and spotless in the sight of God. But the vast majority even of Catholics seem extraordinarily insensible of the venial sins that disfigure their souls and destroy their perfect beauty, and will hardly take any pains to efface these hideous wounds. The fact is, they have no conception of the indescribable filth and fetidness of venial sin, the mere sight of which, we are assured by the saints who have had visions of it, would have stricken them dead with horror were they not divinely sustained.

Let us, at least, stir up the faith that is in us, and look upon venial sin with the eyes of God himself. If only we succeed in doing that, we shall most undoubtedly make frequent use of the many means of effacing them which have been provided us for the purpose, by the immense love and generosity of our divine Redeemer. It is difficult to say which of the two following facts is the most wonderful and astonishing: the generosity and goodness of God in providing us with such a multitude and such a variety of means of purifying ourselves from venial offences; or the apathy and indifference that we show in making full use of them.

If we at all realized the disfigurement, repulsiveness, and hideous deformity of venial sin, in the sight of God and of his unnumbered saints and angels, there can be no doubt but that we would do our utmost to free ourselves from it without a moment's delay. We must all have noticed how carefully people will try and hide (if they cannot remove) any even merely physical disfigurement, and how intensely they object to it being noticed by others. I well remember, many years ago, staying in a certain lordly castle, which was filled with guests. Among them was a young married lady famous for her beauty. But, strange to say, after the first day when she came down to dinner she seemed to disappear, and I saw her no more. On inquiring the cause, I was informed in a whisper that a little pimple or boil, or something of the sort, had come out on the end of her nose. It somewhat detracted from her beauty and she would not come down, but remained a determined prisoner in her room. Nothing would induce her to expose her face to the assembled guests until this little disfigurement could be removed, and she took endless pains and trouble to effect its departure. It was not till her face had recovered its usual beauty that she appeared, after a week's absence.

Surely we may learn a valuable lesson here. If a vain woman will take so much trouble to remove a little physical disfigurement, lest she should be less admired by a few mortals as imperfect as herself, how much more ready and anxious should we be to take trouble, and to exert ourselves to remove from our souls the filth of venial sin, that not only disfigures them, but which renders them immeasurably more hideous and unsightly in the presence of Almighty God and his holy angels than any possible physical defect or distortion. And all the more so, since God's infinite compassion has provided so many different means of washing away our lesser faults, which means are as easy and as simple as they are efficacious. And this brings us to the most practical part of our task.

Let us begin by laying down some general propositions. In the first place, we must be sure that we are not in mortal sin. Though mortal sins may be absolved while the stains of venial offences still remain, yet the converse is not true. For no single venial sin can disappear from the soul until all grievous sins have been forgiven. "Qui est in peccato mortali, caret gratia Dei. Unde nullum veniale ei remittitur."[4]

But supposing the soul to be in a state of grace, then a single sincere act of charity is sufficient to erase all our venial sins, even though we should be unable to call them all to mind, though, of course, not one can be remitted to which we still adhere. St. Thomas clearly teaches that "Nullum peccatum actuale sine contritione remittitur" (No actual sin can be forgiven without contrition). On the other hand, contrition is of such wonderful efficacy and power that it can render us the most marvelous services, which go on increasing and extending according to its greater purity and intensity, till at last, by God's grace, it may attain such depth and strength in the heart of the repentant sinner, as to free him entirely not only from every sin, but also from all the punishment due to it![5].

The great prince of theologians, St. Thomas, points out three different means of obtaining from our loving Lord the remission of our venial offences. For this purpose, he teaches, a fresh infusion of grace is not necessary, but a mere act of sincere contrition, proceeding from the grace which we still have, is quite enough. Thus, *firstly*, to recite with proper dispositions the *Miserere*, the *Confiteor* or the *Pater Noster* will suffice to blot out venial sin.

A *second* method is by the infusion of fresh grace, as, for instance, by means of the Holy Eucharist, and of Extreme Unction, and of the other sacraments of the New Law which are channels of divine grace.

A *third* method is to express our reverence to God and things of God by making use of a sacramental, and thereby obtaining from God the sorrow which will secure forgiveness. Thus the episcopal blessing, the taking of holy water, and, speaking generally, the use of sacramentals, may all be made use of to free our souls from the stains of our daily faults and negligences.[6] For priests especially the beautiful prayer in the holy Mass in which they offer up the sacred Victim, "pro innumerabilibus peccatis et offensionibus et negligentis, etc.," should be said with heartfelt contrition, day by day, as they stand at the Altar of Sacrifice.

Further, as Blosius says, "In satisfaction for our sins, we should offer to God the merits, labors, works, sorrows, and wounds of Christ, for these will, without doubt, avail as *full satisfaction for all our sins*" (*A Book of Spiritual Instruction*, p. 73).

Many souls are deterred from resolutely aiming at perfection, by reason of the long way they think they will have to travel, and because they imagine that it is a task which must take years and years to accomplish. Let us, then, take this opportunity to assure them, in the first place, that so excellent is the end sought after, that we should be well recompensed for all our trouble *even if it did take all our life* to secure it; and that even then our labor would be well expended, for "that which is at present momentary and light of our tribulation worketh for us above measure exceedingly an eternal weight of glory" (2 Cor. 4:17). In the second place, we would remind them that any dilatoriness or sluggishness in getting over the ground must be ascribed, not to the nature of the task, but to our own want of fervor and zeal.

"Any slowness or languor that we may have to complain of must be attributed to ourselves, and to ourselves alone, for we might, if we really wished it, reach the *heights of perfection in a single day, yea, in a single hour*, if, with our whole heart, we turned away from creatures to adhere wholly to God."[7] What a wonderful thought!

This quotation, with several other passages in harmony with it, may be found in the *Compendium Theologiæ Ascetico-Mysticæ*, by Father Josepho Calasanctio Cardinal Vives, O.M.Cap. (pp. 100 and 101, in the note). It is certainly most consoling, and should inspire even the old, who have not much time left, with fresh hope, and with renewed energy in the service of God.

How assiduously we should exercise ourselves in acts of love and contrition! And how earnestly should we crave from God the grace to advance each day in his love, and in sorrow for our faults! What indeed could be more delightful and consoling, when lying on our death-beds and just about to pass before the Judgement-Seat, than the grace to make an act of perfect love, deep enough and strong enough to remove every obstacle and to clear us a free passage to Heaven, without even passing through the purging flames of Purgatory! There are probably very few who are received at once into Paradise, but the reason is because there are few who steadily cultivate and exercise the queenly virtue of charity, and who love to exercise it on every occasion.

Blosius writes: "If a man shall offer himself from pure love, and with perfect resignation to suffer every pain in honor of the divine justice, with a tranquil and willing mind, he will not undergo the pains either of hell or of purgatory, no, not even if he himself had committed all the sins of the whole world" (pp. 143-4). "For, it is certain that any one, who goes out of this world in this state of pure and perfect resignation, will fly immediately to the kingdom of Heaven." He then explains the reason of this, saying: "For, as no kind of pain and no burning of the fire of purgatory can affect God, so neither can it affect a man who is perfectly united to God in conformity of will and love" (p. 143).

Let us, then, take heed not to be thoughtless and remiss in this important matter, but do all in our power so to prepare our souls, that when the last moment of life approaches we may have the unspeakable satisfaction of winging our way, directly and without delay, from earth to Heaven.

4

"Supposing it were possible to convert all heretics, Turks, and Jews to the true faith; to rescue every damned soul from hell, and every suffering soul from Purgatory; and to procure the eternal salvation of every human being that has ever lived or ever will live, by the deliberate commission of one single venial sin, such as a willful distraction, it would be absolutely wrong to commit it. This is certain."—A. Bellecio, S.J. (see Note).[1]

So soon as a man begins thoroughly to realize the enormity of even venial sins, and the great number with which his soul is stained, if he is wise he will not rest quietly, but will at once arouse himself, and seek to do all in his power to atone for them. Because we soil our hands many times a day, we have the habit of washing them again and again. It should be the same with our souls stained by venial sins. As we are continually offending, so we should be continually making satisfaction for them, for we must never forget that every sin, offence, and negligence has its own separate and definite punishment.

That list of penalties increases, silently but surely, every day. As the spendthrift is overwhelmed by a continually greater weight of debt, so are we exposed continually to a greater and greater score of punishments catalogued against us. We may trust that God has forgiven our offences, but the punishment remains. In spite of God's love for us, and recognizing us as his own, he will consign us to Purgatory. There we shall go through our sins once more in their punishment. There we shall suffer, but here is the time for a thorough repentance. Here is the time of good works, of obtaining indulgences, of wiping out the debt in every possible way. The saints, though to the eyes of man without sin, really had a vast account— and they settled it by continual trials here. We have neither their merit nor their sufferings.[2]

Let us, at least, be ready and anxious to make use of such means as are at our disposal.

Among these means, the most obvious is the performance of good works and meritorious actions, which are innumerable and of almost infinite variety. They may be said to embrace every good thought, desire, word, or action that can form part of human activity, when performed in the state of sanctifying grace and from motives of the love of God, according to the teaching of St. Paul, when he writes: "Whether

you eat or drink, or whatsoever else you do, do all to
the glory of God" (1 Cor. 10:13); and again, when writing
to the Colossians (3:17): "All whatsoever you do in word
or in work, all things do ye in the name of our Lord
Jesus Christ, giving thanks to God and the Father by
him."

Indeed, there are few things in which the immense
liberality and generosity of God are so manifested, as
in his manner of rewarding good works. Even if the
only result of these good works were to atone for our
many venial sins, we should have a very strong motive
for performing them, but God in his generosity has
attached to them many other priceless effects. They
not only (1) satisfy for our venial sins, and obtain
(entirely or in part) the remission of the temporal
punishment due to them, but they also (2) increase
sanctifying grace in the soul; (3) add to our power of
impetration or intercession; and (4) increase our
eternal glory in heaven. Let us briefly consider each of
these effects in turn.

The first fruit of every meritorious action which we
perform, while in the grace of God, is its power to
cancel a part or even the whole of the temporal
punishment incurred by the commission of sin. We
shall realize the great importance of this so soon as
ever we call to mind that God has so ordained that
every single sin of our whole lives, even the smallest, is
necessarily and infallibly followed by its appropriate
punishment; and that this punishment must be
endured in all its rigor and completeness before the

soul can be admitted into the unveiled presence of God, and enjoy the beatific Vision.

But though there is no possible escape from this necessity, yet there are two very different ways of meeting it and of paying our debt. We may pay it voluntarily and freely, *in this life*, or we may be forced to pay it, with immeasurably greater agony and suffering, *in the next*. If we have been guilty of many venial, and still more, of course, of forgiven mortal sins, we have every reason to fear that a very large debt of punishment may be in reserve for us in the world beyond the grave. With this thought standing clearly before us, it must surely be a source of immense consolation to know, with all the certainty of divine faith, that the assiduous performance of good works enables us, through the merits of Christ, to satisfy every claim of divine justice.

Moreover, the advantages of choosing to take our punishment in this life rather than in the other are both many and weighty.

1. In the first place, let us comfort ourselves with the thought that, by our earnestness and fervor in the service of God *now*, while we are "in the way," we may succeed in accomplishing, in a comparatively *short time*, what the merciless and tormenting flames of Purgatory might not be able to accomplish in many, many years. Now to shorten, by however little, our detention amid the cleansing flames is a matter of the utmost consequence, for every minute that we are forcibly kept back from enjoying the delights of

Paradise will fill our souls with inexpressible anguish and regret, and seem to be almost an eternity.

2. The second great advantage of paying the penalty of sin in this rather than in the next life arises from the fact that the pains we are called upon to endure in Purgatory, in spite of their being much greater than any we are likely to meet with on earth, serve but only one purpose. They atone for sin, and satisfy the justice of God: and that is all. On the other hand, the voluntary sufferings and the good works we willingly perform on earth, not only atone for sin and satisfy divine justice, but *in addition to this*, they gain new merits for heaven, and keep on adding to the eternal weight of glory awaiting us in our celestial home.

Consider that if I were in Purgatory at this moment, I might be suffering the most prolonged and excruciating pains, yet without meriting any further glory in Heaven, for the very power of meriting is limited to man's life upon earth. On the other hand, while in this life, I may not only pay the penalty of sin with very much less suffering, but will at the same time be acquiring grace and adding to my eternal reward by every act I perform. The full realization of this truth should exert a very strong influence over the whole of my life. In the first place it should impel me to do all the good possible, so long as life lasts; and in the second place, it should dispose me to receive not merely with patience and resignation, but with gratitude and even with positive joy, every cross, trial, suffering, and humiliation which God in his goodness may send me.

3. The third fruit or recompense that God bestows upon us for every good work, no matter how trifling and insignificant, is an increase of sanctifying grace. And one particle of such grace is worth more than a thousand worlds! The spiritual life of the soul may go on increasing and improving without any limit. In material things it is different. A plant or a tree, a bird or a beast, and man himself, so far as his body is concerned, are capable of reaching a certain limited degree of perfection, but then can advance no longer. After attaining their greatest development, no further improvement is possible: in fact, they then begin to deteriorate. But the spiritual life of the soul knows no limitations. So long as man is on his trial, he can continually add and add more and yet more to his spiritual growth. Even though one possessed at the present moment the grace of a seraph or a cherub, one might still go on increasing it and adding to it, every day and every hour, until one's soul quits the body. This is surely worth remembering and pondering over and reducing, as far as possible, to practice. And all the more so, because theologians assure us that God loves his creatures in a greater and yet greater degree according to the greater measure of sanctifying grace that they possess.

There is nothing in the wide world that we should so esteem or long for, as the love of God: yet to increase in sanctifying grace is, at the same time, and *pari passu*, to draw down upon ourselves a larger share of his love. And every increase of sanctifying grace increases that love still further. It is difficult for any of us to realize with what inexpressible tenderness God loves a soul having even the very lowest degree of sanctifying grace. Who then shall attempt to describe his love for one, who has spent long years, yea, perhaps his entire life in the steady practice of virtue and holiness, and the diligent and uninterrupted performance of every kind of meritorious action! And who would not count any trouble or suffering cheap, if thereby he could secure a larger share in God's affection, which, through God's inconceivable generosity and goodness, he may now do so easily and so continually!

4. But we have by no means exhausted the marvelous fruits arising from good works performed in a state of grace. The fourth fruit which we may mention is the increase of impetratory power merited by such actions. Every soul in grace is dear to Almighty God, and he most graciously opens his ears to even the least worthy of them. As we read in the Psalms, "The eyes of the Lord are upon the just, and his ears unto their prayers" (Ps. xxxiii 16). But, if he listens to all most readily, he is far more easily moved by the prayers of those who love him most, and who are anxious at all times to please him and to do his will. In short, the greater the saint the greater the impetratory power he yields. We are all God's debtors, and he is always answering our prayers and granting our petitions, but when we read the lives of his saints, we at once note

that they ask for and obtain many marvelous favors which would never be granted to us, and which we could never even ask for, without the greatest presumption. Because the saints were so exalted in virtue, and had acquired such a wealth of sanctifying grace, God brought about the most extraordinary conversions in answer to their prayers, and cured the sick and raised the dead again and again, when they called upon him. There is no one whose prayers are more efficacious than those of the Immaculate Mother of God, because she exceeds all other saints in sanctity; but other saints wield a greater or a lesser power, in proportion to their holiness. We have many wonderful examples in the Old Testament, such as those of Abraham, Moses, Elias, Zachary, Jacob, and Stephen and many others, all of whom were reckoned as special favorites of God, by reason of their singular virtue and of the amount of sanctifying grace which adorned their souls. In a word, their immense love of God constrained him to shower his choicest blessings upon them and readily to grant extraordinary favors, for which ordinary imperfect mortals might have asked in vain.

5. Though other fruits arise from the performance of good works, we will now limit ourselves to the consideration of but one more, which is perhaps the most magnificent of all. We refer to the increase of our eternal glory in Heaven. There is nothing greater or more precious to which we can aspire. There is nothing which the saints valued so highly, or for which

they were more ready to suffer and endure. Take a single instance; weigh well these words of St. Teresa. She says: "I say that if I were asked which I preferred, either to endure all the trials of the world until the end of it, and then receive *one slight degree* of glory additional, or else, without any suffering of any kind to enter into glory of a *slightly lower degree*, I would accept —oh, how willingly—all those trials for one slight degree of fruition in the contemplation of the greatness of God; for I know that he who understands him best, loves and praises him best."[3] Now, this additional degree of glory for the sake of which St. Teresa declares herself willing to endure the trials and troubles of the world, all through the ages, down to the day of judgement, we may secure by each and every one of our good actions, if performed according to the conditions of merit. For, in the first place, each of these actions secures for us an increase of grace, and each increase of grace carries with it a corresponding claim to a further increase of eternal glory in Heaven, which means that God will be more fully known, more perfectly possessed, more ardently loved, and more intensely enjoyed for the whole of eternity. No mortal man can have the faintest idea of the full meaning of these words. They mean immeasurably more than any human being, in this life, can either imagine or conceive. They mean what eye hath not seen, what ear hath not heard, and all those inexpressible and endless joys that it hath not entered into the heart of man to conceive, but which God has prepared for those who love him.

Whatever may be our present claim to eternal glory, even though it were that of the highest of the archangels, we can still go on, day by day, and hour by hour, increasing and extending it still further, by every meritorious action, so long as life lasts. Let us take an example. The *Angelus* bell is ringing; instead of paying no attention, we kneel down, and devoutly recite the *Angelus*; or we are troubled with a sharp toothache, but instead of complaining, we suffer it with perfect resignation, and offer our pain to God, in satisfaction for our sins; or a beggar comes and solicits alms, and instead of closing our ear to his piteous tale, we drop a few pence into his extended hand, for love of Christ, who became poor that he might enrich us; or we hear of some acquaintance taken ill, and instead of dismissing the thought, we go and console and comfort him, and help him in his misery. Such easy and simple acts may be multiplied almost without end, yet each and every one of them, if the ordinary conditions are verified, produces an effect perfectly bewildering to contemplate. Each will most infallibly procure for us, what St. Teresa declared she would (were it necessary) be willing to purchase, by enduring all the sufferings of the world to the end of time, namely, a real increase of eternal glory. Surely, with such possibilities before us, we should bestir ourselves, and (to use Faber's expression) keep on "minting money for Heaven," so long as life lasts.

Just pause for a moment to reflect upon the stupendous weight of eternal glory that will fall to the portion of a really careful, energetic and indefatigable laborer in the vineyard of the Church, who deliberately and systematically lays himself out to profit by every possible opportunity that chances to arise, and who, like a good husbandman, never loses a chance of bettering his position and of adding to his spiritual riches. We are especially commanded by our Lord not to bury our talent in the ground, but rather to trade with it until he comes, and to turn it to the very best possible account. For if every single good work carries with it such magnificent rewards, how marvelously large and measureless must be the collective rewards of the many millions of meritorious actions that can easily be performed before the cold hand of death puts a final limit to our activity. Though the multitude of meritorious actions may, if our life be a long one, defy all calculations, yet we must remember that not a single one, even though the most insignificant, will be overlooked or forgotten. For God, who loves us more than we can say, is not willing that we should forfeit even the least degree of glory to which we have acquired a right. We may all say quite as confidently as the glorious St. Paul himself: "I know whom I have trusted, and I am certain that he is able to keep that which I have committed to him, against that day" (of eternity) (2 Tim. 1:12).

If a man were to arise, in any part of the world, who could in very truth show men how they might easily and with absolute certainty increase their incomes, double their profits, and grow speedily enormously rich in this world's goods, what vast crowds of earnest excited people would immediately crowd around him, and hang upon his lips. All sorts and conditions of men would long to learn his secret, and yearn with the utmost impatience to profit by it. It would be quite impossible to describe the feverish eagerness, unflagging energy, and the endless trouble they would all show to put his advice into practice, and to get their coffers filled with the precious metal!

Yet—to our eternal shame, be it said—when a minister of God arises to tell them how easily, and yet how infallibly they may heap up for themselves treasures of an infinitely superior kind, and immeasurably more precious than gold, and far more joy-wielding and incomparably more enduring, few will pay the slightest attention, or deem it worth their while either to listen to his instructions or to follow his counsel. This is the more extraordinary, because the preacher is but a messenger of the Lord of Heaven and of earth, whose authority and power and generosity exceed all limit. For it is no other than our divine Master, who bids us not to trouble to "lay up to ourselves treasures on earth, where the rust and the moth consume, and where thieves break through and steal," but "to lay up treasures for ourselves in Heaven, where neither the rust nor the moth consume, and where thieves do not break through nor steal" (Matt. 6:19).

How astonishing, and at the same time how

terribly distressing it is to witness even good, honest men actually throwing away golden chances, and absolutely neglecting the most splendid opportunities, which will never return, and losing, from sheer carelessness, countless spiritual treasures, for which the saints would have cheerfully given all they possessed, and would have made any sacrifice to obtain.

Inexpressibly sad though this be, yet it does but prove the eternal truth enunciated by St. Luke, viz., that "the children of this world are wiser in their generation than the children of light" (16:8). Let us at least learn wisdom from the practical common sense of the children of this world, and eagerly seize and turn to account the many admirable chances that God continually puts in our way of enriching our heavenly inheritance more and more as life wears on. Alas for our blindness! The prophet may well declare that "When man was in honor he did not understand it; he hath been compared to senseless beasts, and is become like to them" (Ps. 48:13). With the same inspired writer we may well say: "Let us not become like the horse and the mule, who have no understanding" (Ps. 31:9), but let us rather act with all the prudence and zeal of enlightened children of an infinitely loving Father, who desires to welcome us one day to a very high place in his eternal Home.

NOTES

Chapter 1

1. Vide Anglican Difficulties, p. 19
2. Rom. xi 33.

Chapter 2

1. Witness of the Saints, p. 32.
2. Discourses to Mixed Cong., p. 34.
3. Vide Newman, Disc. to Mixed Cong., pp. 338 et seq.

Chapter 3

1. When I was a student in Rome, the famous theologian Ballerini, S.J., used to speak highly of Frassinetti, and strongly recommended us to study his Compendio della Teologia Morale. Now, this is what Frassinetti writes regarding venial sin (Tratto xvii nota 126): "The doctrine of the Council of Trent regarding venial sins, that is that due to human weakness, they cannot all be avoided throughout the entire course of life without a special privilege from the Lord, should be understood to refer to venial sins that are barely noticed; because fully deliberate venial sins, that is, those committed with one's eyes wide open and with full knowledge of their maliciousness, can all be equally avoided just as mortal sins can, as Saint Alphonsus de' Liguori precisely teaches."
2. Méditations Sacerdotales, vol. i., pp. 375-6.
3. See The Golden Key, p. 55, by Rev. P. Griffith, C.SS.R.
4. St. Thomas
5. "Perfect contrition, whether considered on the part of charity or on the part of sensible sorrow, can grow to such an extent that it suffices for the full erasure of guilt and punishment; as is evident

from the example of the Good Thief." (vide P. Clément Marc, C.SS.R., vol. ii., No. 1674, p. 218).

6. "Hence, for three reasons, certain things cause the remission of venial sins: first, because they imply the infusion of grace, since the infusion of grace removes venial sins, as stated above; and so, by the Eucharist, Extreme Unction, and by all the sacraments of the New Law without exception, wherein grace is conferred, venial sins are remitted. Secondly, because they imply a movement of detestation for sin, and in this way the general confession [*i.e. the recital of the Confiteor or of an act of contrition], the beating of one's breast, and the Lord's Prayer conduce to the remission of venial sins, for we ask in the Lord's Prayer: 'Forgive us our trespasses.' Thirdly, because they include a movement of reverence for God and Divine things; and in this way a bishop's blessing, the sprinkling of holy water, any sacramental anointing, a prayer said in a dedicated church, and anything else of the kind, conduce to the remission of venial sins." (Summa Theologica, P. 3, Q. lxxxvii., Art. 3, p. 586).

7. This, at least, is the teaching of Cardinal Vives and of Marotius, whom he quotes with approval, in the following remarkable words: "It must be said that all delay and procrastination in our progress comes from ourselves. For if we wish, we can, IN ONE DAY, NAY, EVEN IN A SINGLE HOUR, reach the height of holiness, if with all our heart, turning away from creatures, we turn to God."

Chapter 4

1. "Si unicâ distractione omnes hæreticos, Turcas et Gentiles ad veram fidem convertere; si omnes damnatos ex inferno, omnes purgantes animas ex purgatorio liberare; si omnes, qui vivunt, vel vivent homines æternæ salutis securas reddere possem, non liceret. . . . Hoc certum est. Nam omnia hæc mala non nisi creaturæ mala sunt; peccatum verò, etiam veniale, malum Dei est. QUANTUM DISTAT CREATURA A CREATORE, TANTUM MALITIA HUJUS SUPERAT MALIGNITATEM ALTIORIS" (A. Bellecio, S.J., in Triduum Sacrum Religio sorum usui Accommodatum, pp. 8, 9).

2. See Newman's Meditations and Devotions, p. 471.

3. Life of St. Teresa, chap. xxxvii., sec. 3.